PIANO / VOCAL / GUITAR

train

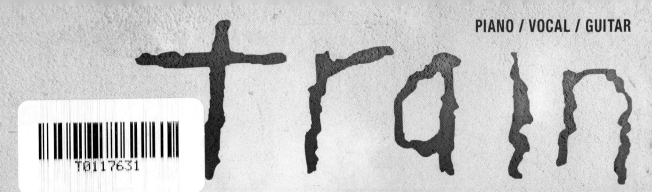

PIANO SHEET MUSIC COLLECTION

ISBN 978-1-4950-2970-7

HAL•LEONARD®
CORPORATION
7777 W. BLUEMOUND RD. P.O. BOX 13819 MILWAUKEE, WI 53213

In Australia Contact:
Hal Leonard Australia Pty. Ltd.
4 Lentara Court
Cheltenham, Victoria, 3192 Australia
Email: ausadmin@halleonard.com.au

Visit Hal Leonard Online at
www.halleonard.com

ANGEL IN BLUE JEANS

Words and Music by AMUND BJØRKLUND,
ESPEN LIND and PAT MONAHAN

Moderate Pop
A5
C5
G5
Oh.
Oh.
mf
D
A5
And though I nev - er got her name
Late that night she got a - way,
C5
G5
or time to find out an - y - thing, I loved her just
I chased her to the turn - pike and lost her where the

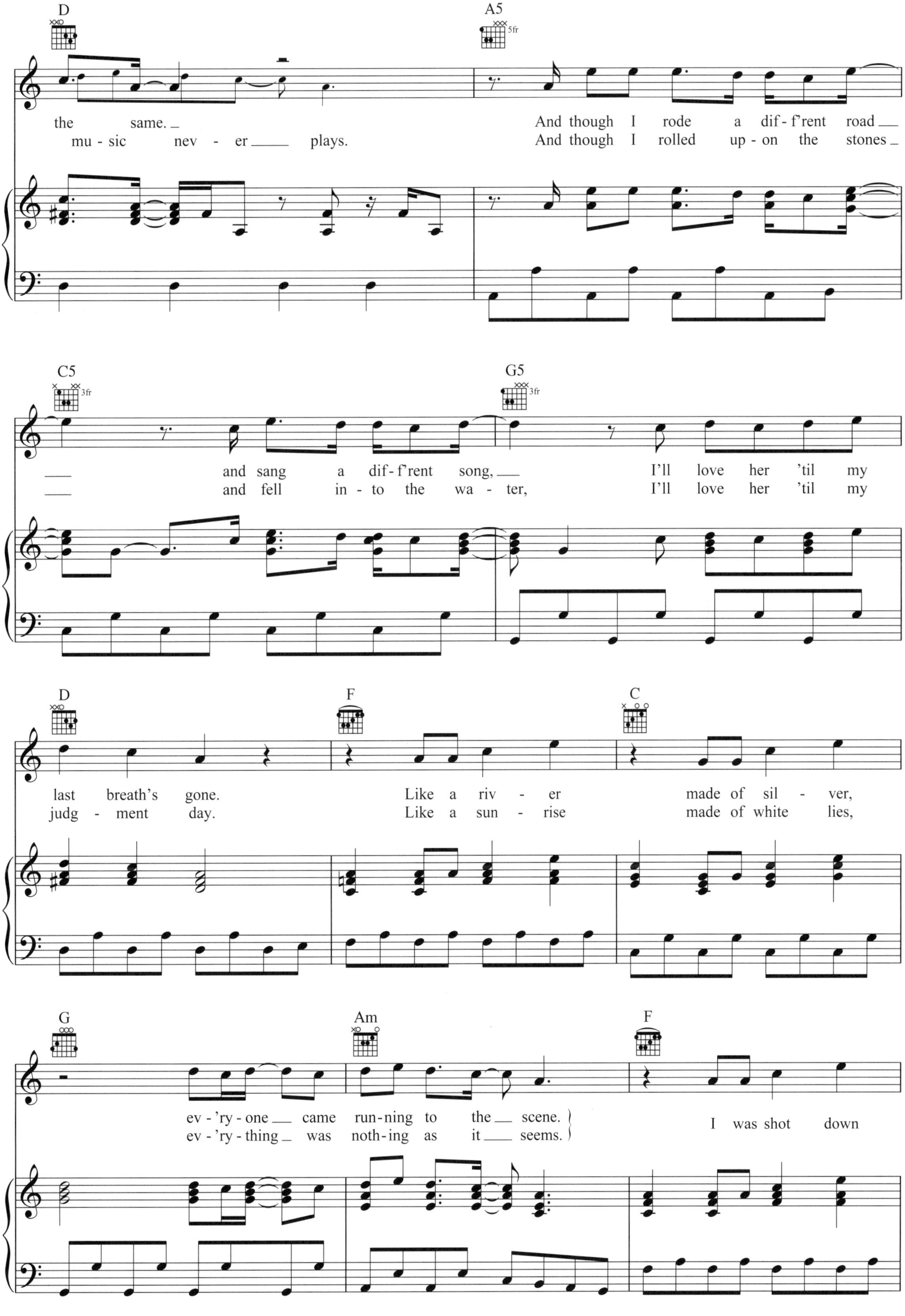
D
A5
5fr
the same.
mu - sic nev - er plays.
And though I rode a dif - f'rent road
And though I rolled up - on the stones
C5
3fr
G5
3fr
and sang a dif - f'rent song,
and fell in - to the wa - ter,
I'll love her 'til my
I'll love her 'til my
D
F
C
last breath's gone.
judg - ment day.
Like a riv - er
Like a sun - rise
made of sil - ver,
made of white lies,
G
Am
F
ev - 'ry - one came run - ning to the scene.
ev - 'ry - thing was noth - ing as it seems.
I was shot down

C
Dm
E7
in cold blood by an an - gel in blue jeans. Oh.
Am
C
G
Hey! Oh.
1
F
Am
Hey!
2
F
Am
Oh.

C
G
F
Oh.
Hey!
G
Dm
F
I hear voic - es call - ing all a - round, I keep fall - ing down. I
Am
G
Dm
think my heart could pound right out of me. I see a mil - lion dif - f'rent ways to
F
Esus
E
nev - er leave this maze a - live.

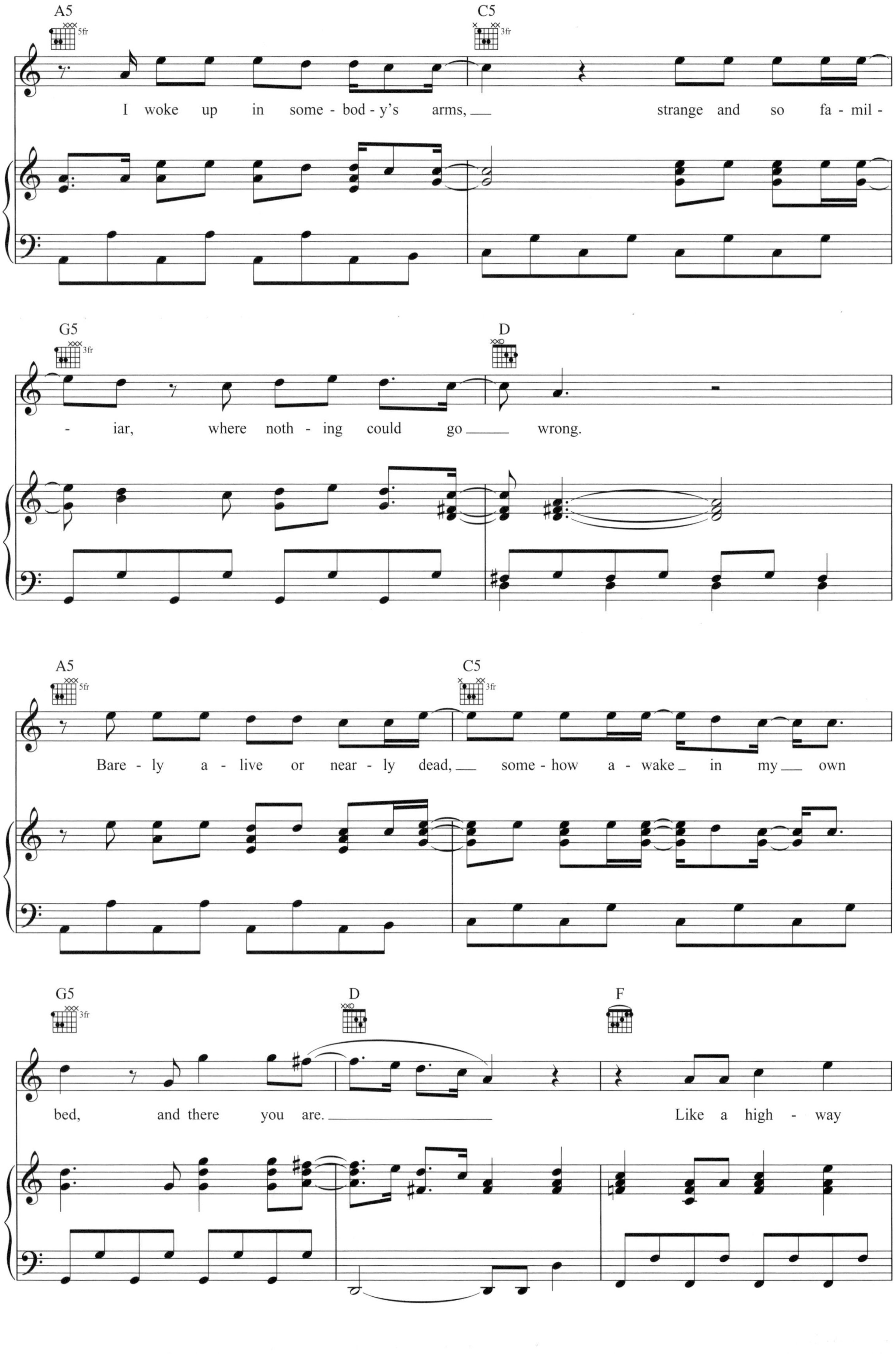
A5
5fr
C5
3fr
I woke up in some - bod - y's arms, strange and so fa - mil -
G5
3fr
D
- iar, where noth - ing could go wrong.
A5
5fr
C5
3fr
Bare - ly a - live or near - ly dead, some - how a - wake in my own
G5
3fr
D
F
bed, and there you are. Like a high - way

C
G
Am
head-ed my way,
life is __ but a dream. ____
F
C
Dm
I was shot down
by your __ love,
my an-gel in blue __
E7
Am
C
__ jeans. ____
Oh. ____
Hey!
G
F
Am
Oh. ____
Oh. ____

C
G
F
Oh.
Oh.
Am
C
G
Hey!
Oh.
F
Am
C
Oh.
Oh.
G
F
Am
Hey!
molto rit.

BULLETPROOF PICASSO

Words and Music by BUTCH WALKER,
PAT MONAHAN, TRENT MAZUR
and MICHAEL FREESH

D Em Csus2 G
an - y - thing I feel? Just be glad I'm real, glad I'm real. Am I
an - y - thing at all. I'm just glad you're here, glad you're real. Are you
D Em C G
real? Are you made of lead paint, a
real? Am I made of tim - ber?
D Em C G
bul - let - proof Pi - cas - so? All the vir - gin saints put you
'Cause I'm on fire. Will you re - mem - ber to -
D Em C G
here to care for me. I don't need a rea - son for
night for ver - y long? You don't need to sell me on

D Em C G/B Am
ev - 'ry - thing I feel; just be glad I say what I mean and
an - y - thing at all; just say what you mean and
C G/B Am G D G
mean what I say to you.
mean what you say to me.
We don't need a
C6 G D Em7
rea - son for an - y - thing we feel. We don't need a
C6 G D Em7
rea - son. Pi - cas - so's at the wheel. So

C G D Em7
roll this top down, hell with this town, leave our bags be-hind. We don't need a
1
C6 G D Em7
rea - son, 'cause I got you and you got me to-night.
C G D Em C G
D Em
Did you ev-er see the
2
C6 G
rea - son, 'cause

D
Dsus2
Em
I got you and you got me to - night. Am - ber waves of grain
C
D(add4)
3fr
fly by high - way lanes. Wait - ing for this change
G5
3fr
G5/F♯
Em
seems like my en - tire life. If on - ly the good die young,
C
D(add4)
3fr
we'll out - last ev - 'ry - one for some of the things we've done.

N.C.
C
G
And we've just be - gun.
D
Em
C6
G
We don't need a rea - son for
D
Em7
C6
G
an - y - thing we feel. We don't need a rea - son. Pi -
D
Em7
C
G
cas - so's at the wheel. So roll this top down, hell with this town, leave

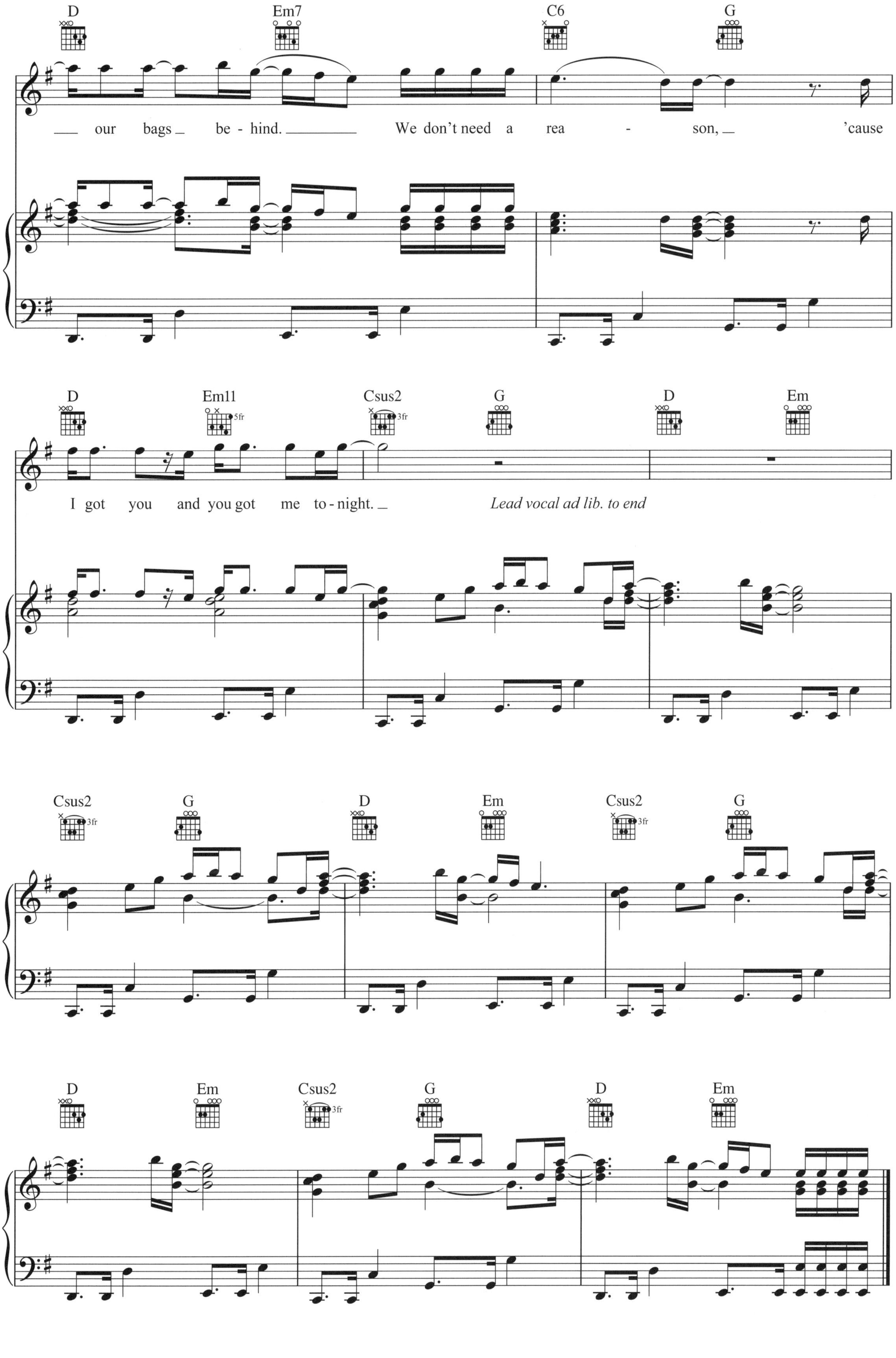
D Em7 C6 G
our bags be - hind. We don't need a rea - son, 'cause
D Em11 Csus2 G D Em
5fr
3fr
I got you and you got me to - night.
Lead vocal ad lib. to end
Csus2 G D Em Csus2 G
3fr
3fr
D Em Csus2 G D Em
3fr

BRUISES

Words and Music by PAT MONAHAN,
ESPEN LIND and AMUND BJØRKLUND

Moderate Country beat

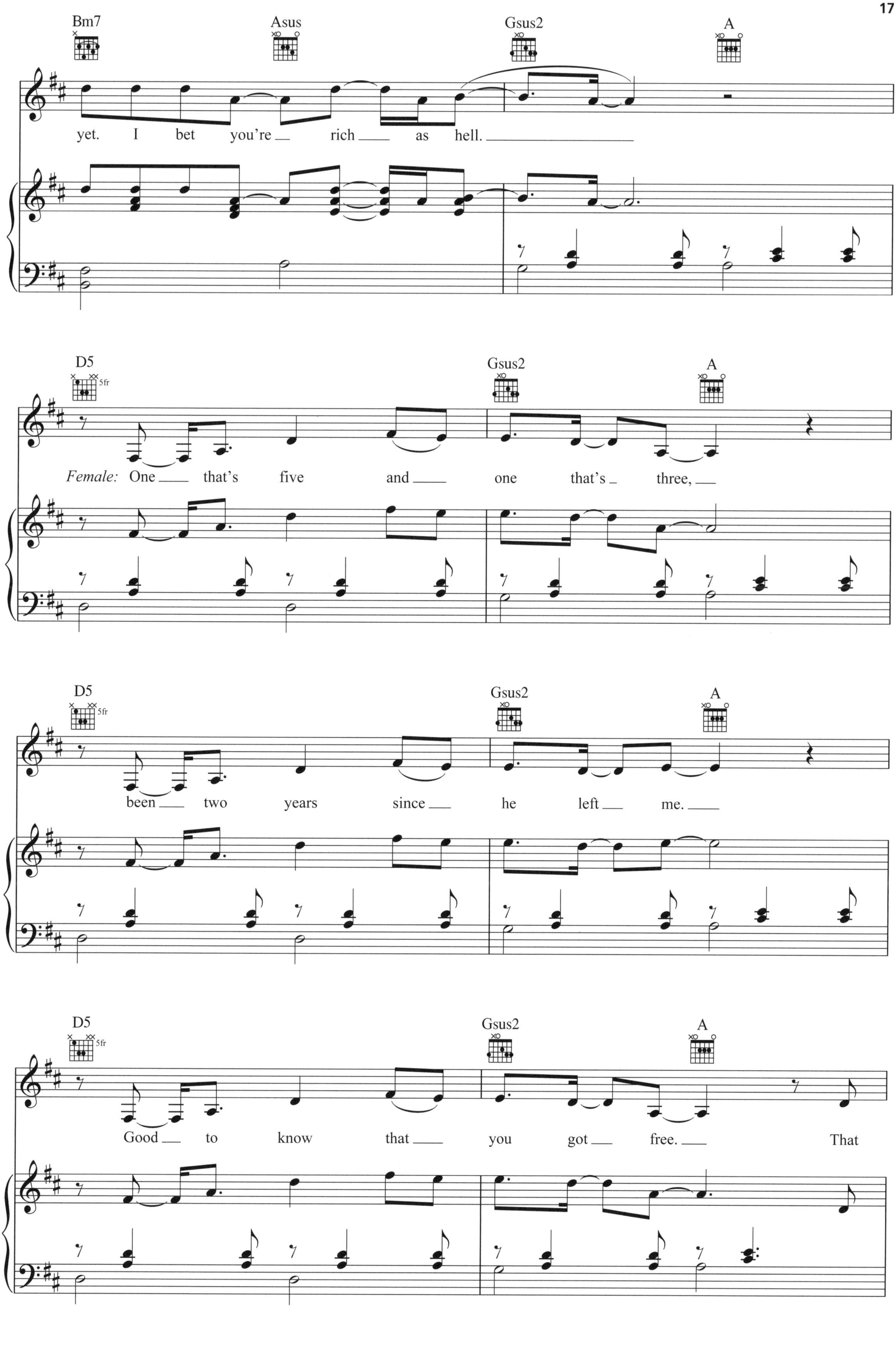
Bm7
Asus
Gsus2
A
yet. I bet you're rich as hell.
D5
5fr
Gsus2
A
Female: One that's five and one that's three,
D5
5fr
Gsus2
A
been two years since he left me.
D5
5fr
Gsus2
A
Good to know that you got free. That

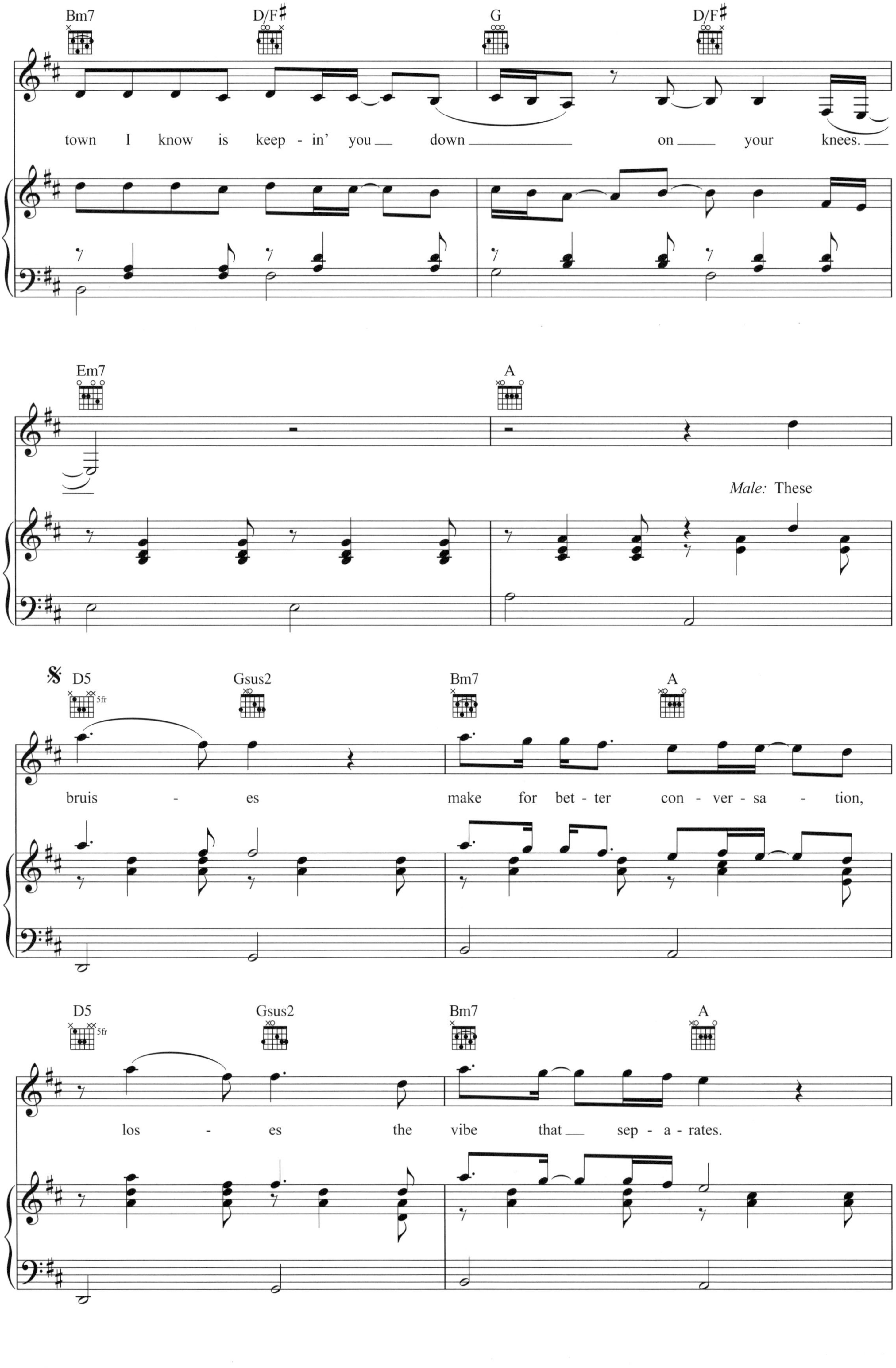
Bm7 D/F♯ G D/F♯
town I know is keep - in' you down on your knees.
Em7 A
Male: These
D5 Gsus2 Bm7 A
5fr
bruis - es make for bet - ter con - ver - sa - tion,
D5 Gsus2 Bm7 A
5fr
los - es the vibe that sep - a - rates.

Gsus2 A F♯/A♯ 4fr Bm
Both: It's good to let you in a - gain. You're not a - lone in how you've been.
Em D/F♯ G A
Ev - 'ry - bod - y los - es, we all got
D Gsus2 Bm7 A
bruis - es. Male: We all got
D Gsus2 Bm7 A
bruis - es.
To Coda

D5
5fr
Gsus2
A
Have you seen him?
Female:
Not in years.
D5
5fr
Gsus2
A
How 'bout her?
Male:
No, but I hear
D5
5fr
Gsus2
A
she's in Queens with the man of her dreams.
Bm7
D/F♯
G
A
Female:
Fun - ny, back then she said that a - bout you.

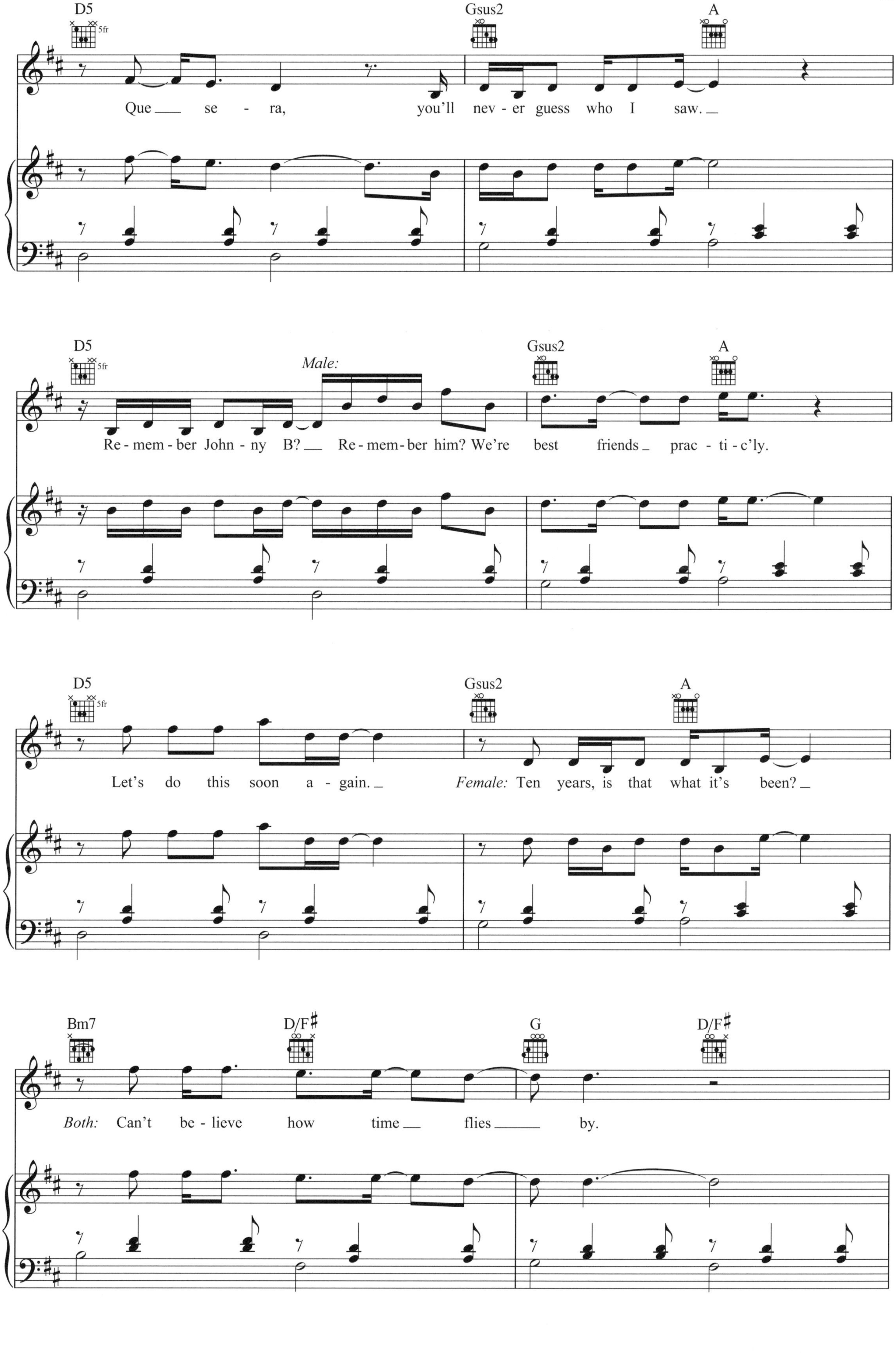
D5
Gsus2
A
5fr
Que — se - ra, you'll nev - er guess who I saw. —
D5
Male:
Gsus2
A
5fr
Re - mem - ber John - ny B? — Re - mem - ber him? We're best friends — prac - ti - c'ly.
D5
Gsus2
A
5fr
Let's do this soon a - gain. —
Female: Ten years, is that what it's been? —
Bm7
D/F♯
G
D/F♯
Both: Can't be - lieve how time — flies — by.

Em
A
D.S. al Coda
Male: Leav - in' you makes me wan - na cry.
Both: These
CODA
Gsus2
A
D/F♯
Gsus2
D/F♯
Male: I would love to fix it all for you.
Em
A
D5
5fr
F♯
Female: I would love to fix you too.
Gsus2
A
Bm
D
Both: Please don't fix a thing what - ev - er you do.

E
D5
Gsus2
Male: These bruis - es
Bm7
A
D5
Gsus2
Bm7
A
make for bet-ter con-ver-sa - tion, los - es the vibe that sep-a-rates.
Gsus2
A
F♯/A♯
Bm
It's good to know you've got a friend that you re-mem-ber now and then.
Em
D/F♯
G
A
Ev - 'ry-bod - y los - es. Both: These

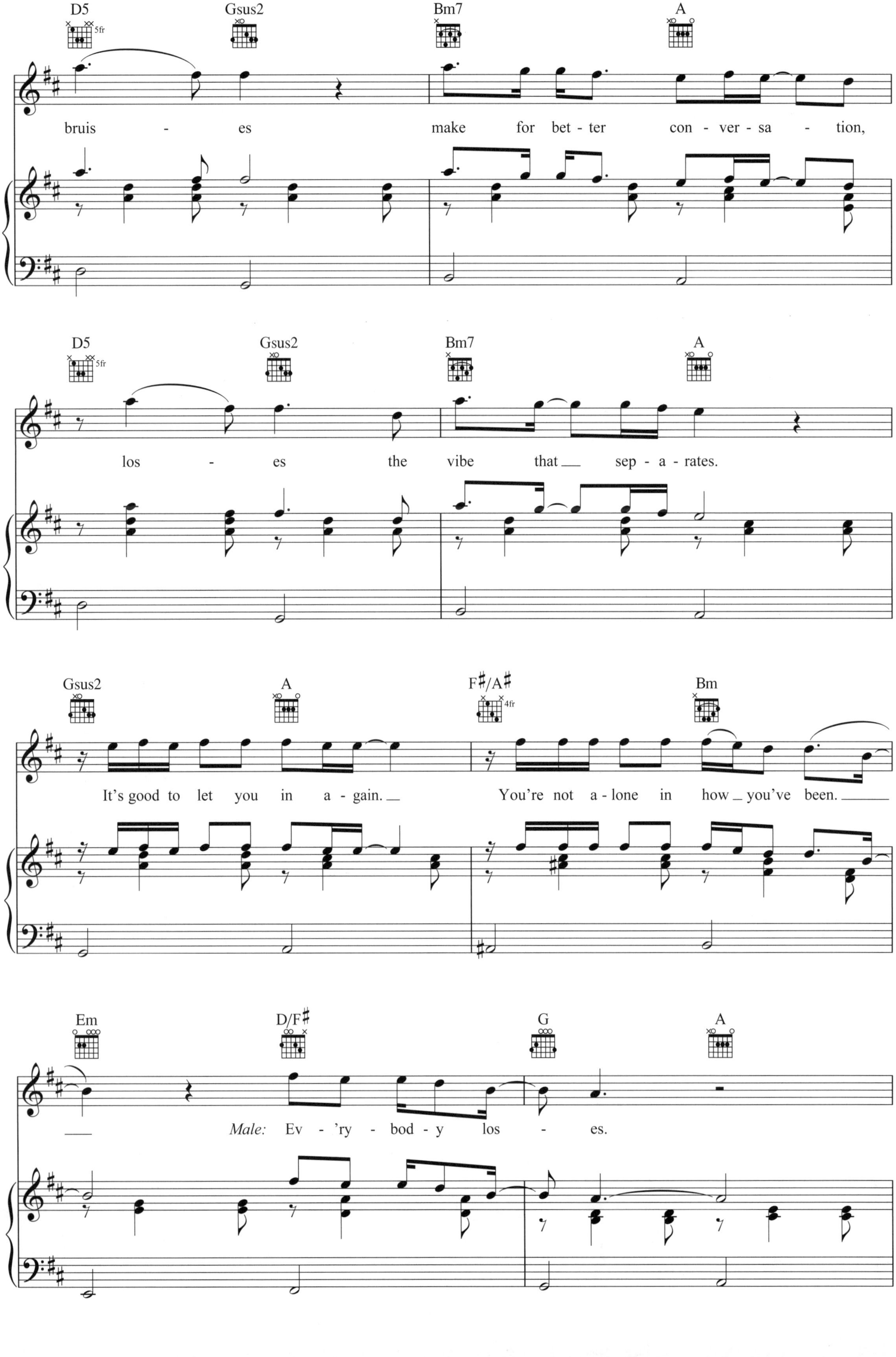
D5
Gsus2
Bm7
A
5fr
bruis - es make for bet - ter con - ver - sa - tion,
D5
Gsus2
Bm7
A
5fr
los - es the vibe that sep - a - rates.
Gsus2
A
F♯/A♯
Bm
4fr
It's good to let you in a - gain. You're not a - lone in how you've been.
Em
D/F♯
G
A
Male: Ev - 'ry - bod - y los - es.

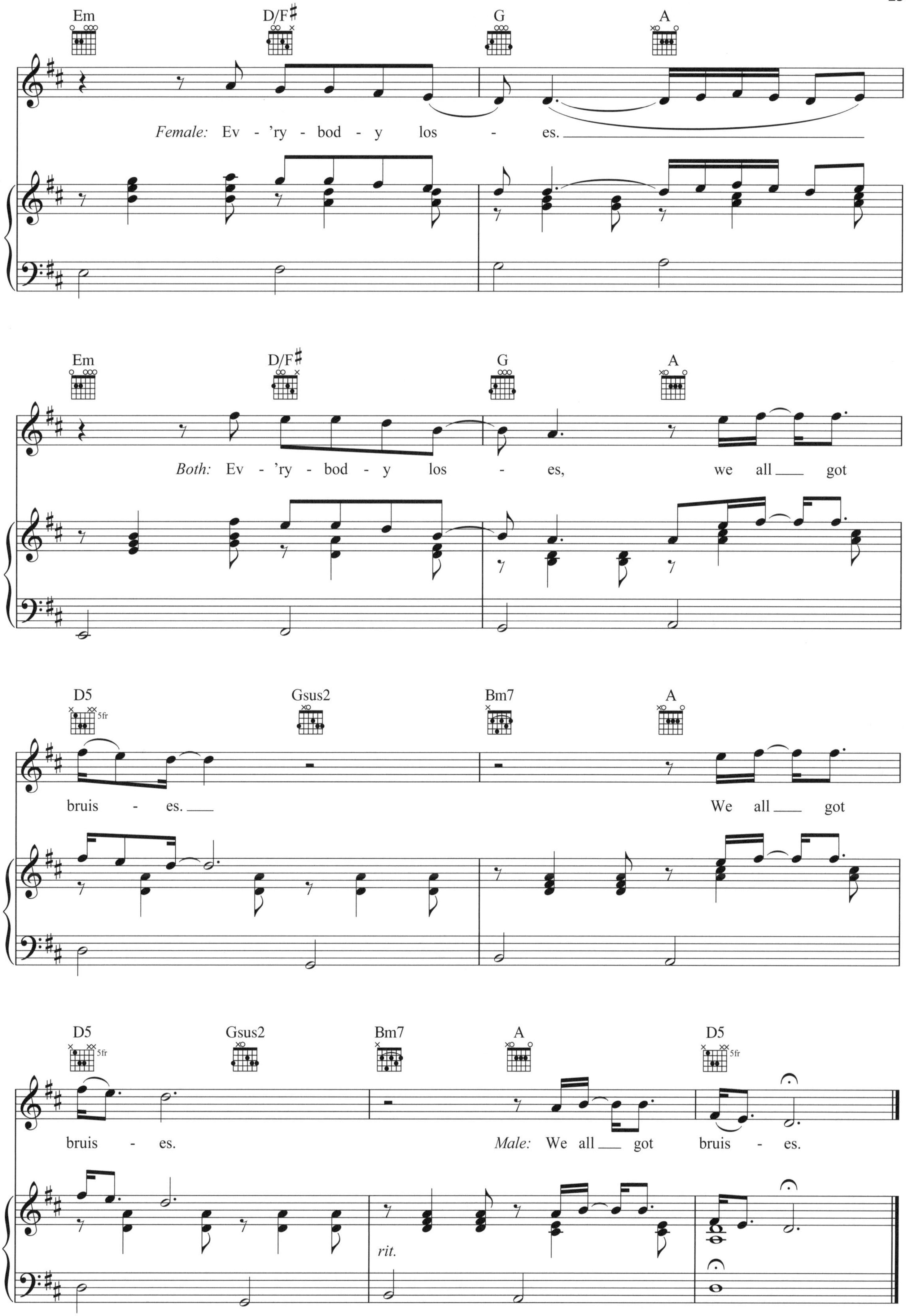

Em
D/F♯
G
A
Female: Ev - 'ry - bod - y los - es.
Em
D/F♯
G
A
Both: Ev - 'ry - bod - y los - es, we all got
D5
5fr
Gsus2
Bm7
A
bruis - es.
We all got
D5
5fr
Gsus2
Bm7
A
D5
5fr
bruis - es.
Male: We all got bruis - es.
rit.

CALLING ALL ANGELS

Words and Music by PAT MONAHAN,
SCOTT UNDERWOOD, JAMES STAFFORD
and CHARLIE COLIN

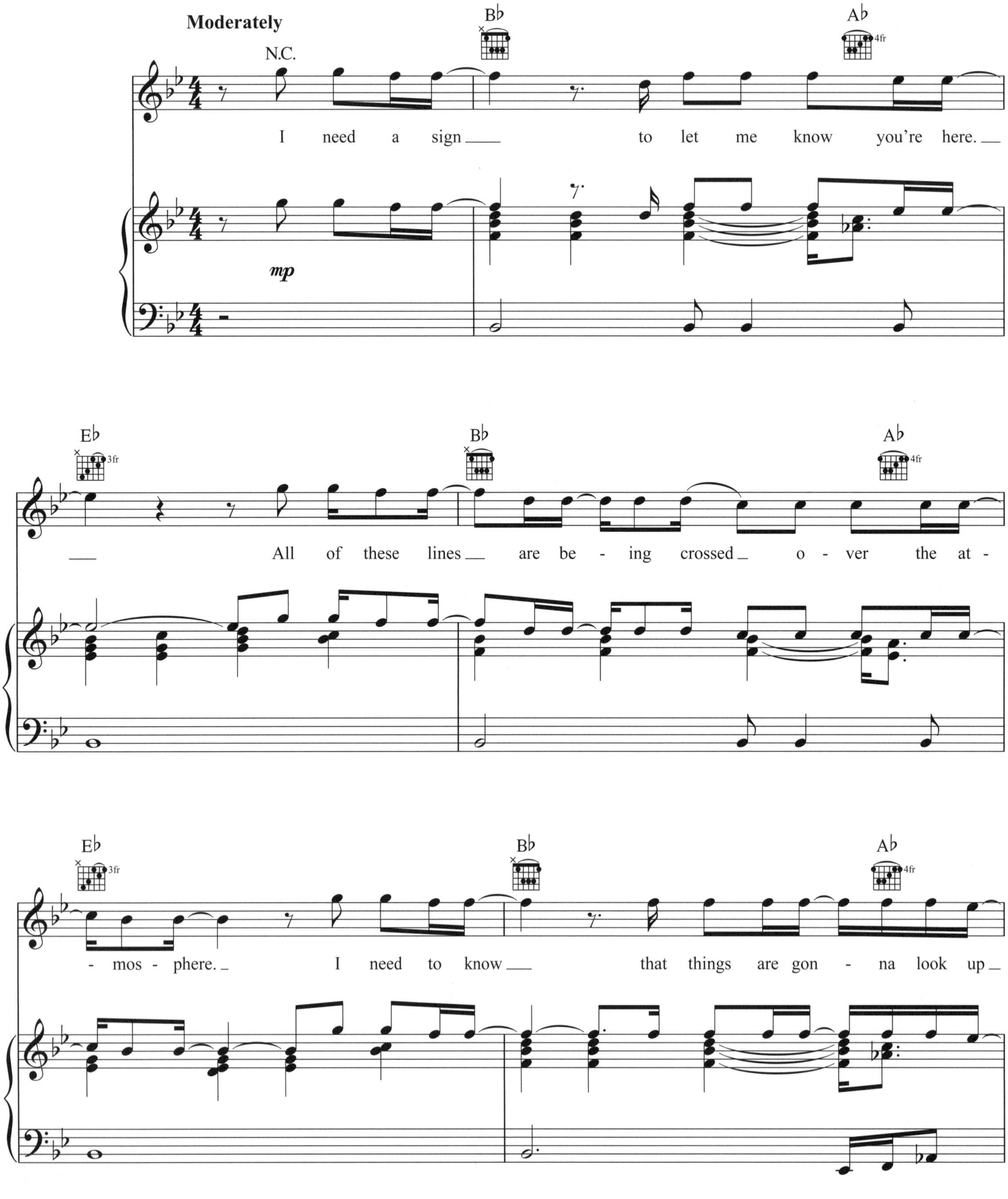
Moderately
N.C.
B♭
A♭
4fr
I need a sign to let me know you're here.
mp
E♭
3fr
B♭
A♭
4fr
All of these lines are be - ing crossed o - ver the at -
E♭
3fr
B♭
A♭
4fr
- mos - phere. I need to know that things are gon - na look up

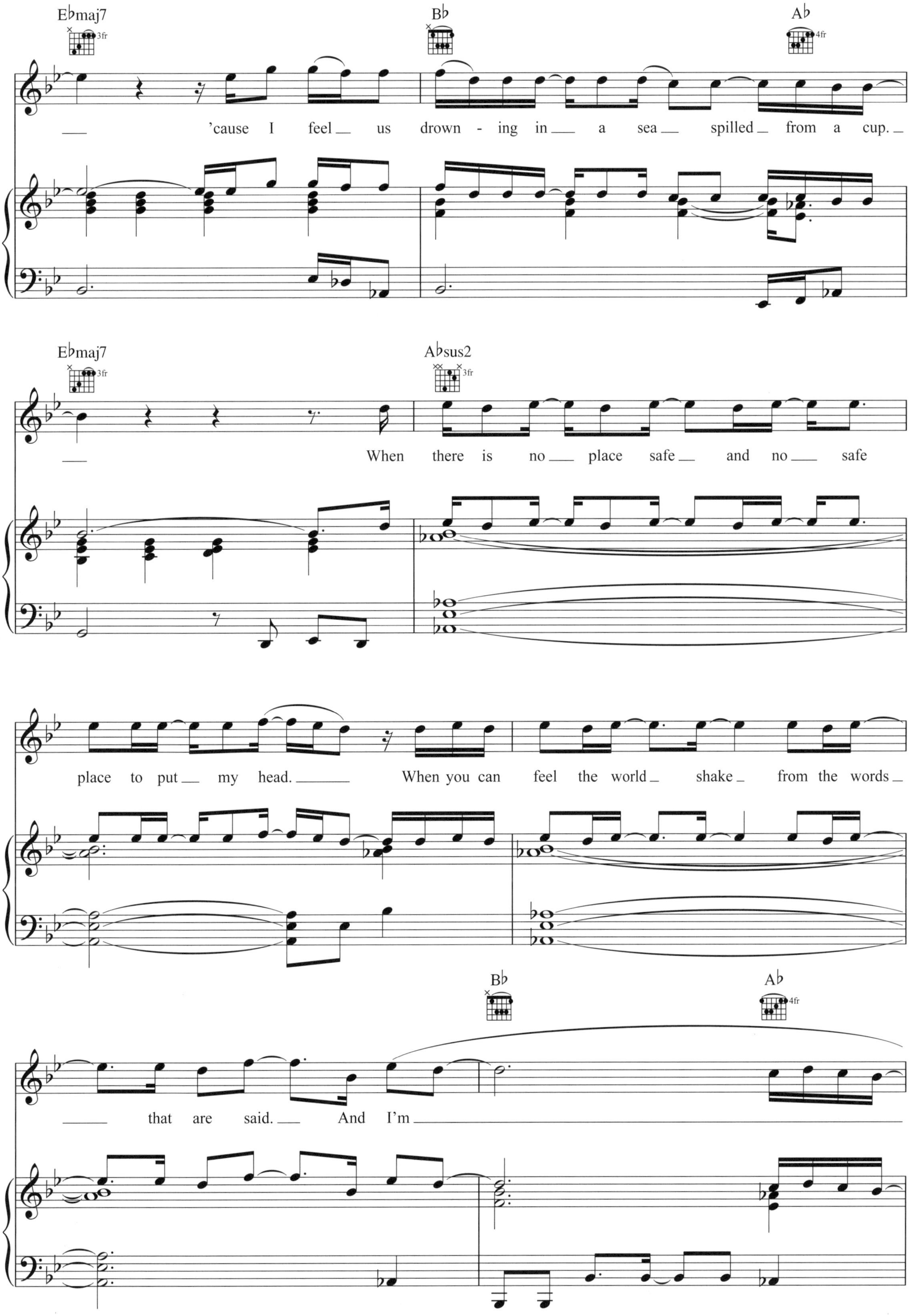
E♭maj7
3fr
B♭
A♭
4fr
'cause I feel us drown - ing in a sea spilled from a cup.
E♭maj7
3fr
A♭sus2
3fr
When there is no place safe and no safe
place to put my head. When you can feel the world shake from the words
B♭
A♭
4fr
that are said. And I'm

E♭
A♭
B♭
A♭
call - ing all an - gels.
E♭/G
Fm
B♭
A♭
And I'm
E♭
A♭
B♭
A♭
call - ing all you an - gels.

E♭/G
A♭sus2
3fr
And I won't give up if you don't give
B♭5
up. I won't give up if you don't give
Cm
up. I won't give up if you don't give
D♭
up. I won't give up if you don't give

B♭
A♭
4fr
up. I need a sign to let me know you're here
E♭/B♭
6fr
B♭
A♭
4fr
'cause my T - V set just keeps it all from be - ing clear.
E♭/G
3fr
Fm
B♭
A♭
4fr
I want a rea - son for the way things have to be.
E♭/B♭
6fr
A♭
4fr
B♭
A♭
4fr
I need a hand to help build up some kind of hope

E♭/G
B♭
A♭
3fr
4fr
in - side of me. And I'm
E♭
B♭
A♭
3fr
4fr
call - ing all an - gels.
E♭/G
Fm
B♭
A♭
3fr
4fr
And I'm

E♭
B♭
A♭
To Coda
calling all you angels.
E♭/G
A♭sus2
When children have to play inside so
they don't disappear, while
B♭5
private eyes solve marriage lies 'cause
we don't talk for years. And
Cm
football teams are kissing queens and

D♭
los-ing sight of hav - ing dreams in a world where what we want is on - ly what we want
N.C.
un - til it's ours.
D.S. al Coda
And I'm
CODA
E♭/G
3fr
Fm
B♭
A♭
4fr
And I'm
(I won't give up if you don't give

E♭
3fr
A♭
4fr
B♭
A♭
4fr
call - ing all an - gels.
up.)
(I won't give up if you don't give
E♭/G
3fr
Fm
B♭
A♭
4fr
And I'm
up.)
(I won't give up if you don't give
E♭
3fr
A♭
4fr
B♭
A♭
4fr
call - ing all you an - gels.
up.)
(I won't give up if you don't give

Repeat and Fade
E♭/G
3fr
Fm
B♭
A♭
4fr
Call - ing all you an - gels.
up.)
(I won't give up if you don't give
E♭
3fr
A♭
4fr
B♭
A♭
4fr
Call - ing all you an - gels.
up.)
(I won't give up if you don't give
E♭/G
3fr
Fm
Optional Ending
B♭
Call - ing all you an - - gels.
up.)

DRIVE BY

Words and Music by PAT MONAHAN,
ESPEN LIND and AMUND BJØRKLAND

E
B
3
wher - ev - er, to get a - way from me.
get down to "more than friends" at last.
F♯m
A
Oh, but that one night was more than just right.
Oh, but that one night was still the high - light.
C♯m
B
F♯m
4fr
I did - n't leave you 'cause I was all through. Oh, I was o - ver - whelmed
I did - n't need you un - til I came to. And I was o - ver - whelmed
A
G♯sus
G♯
and, frank - ly, scared as hell be - cause I real - ly fell for you.

A E B
Oh, I swear to you
(D.S.) oh, I swear to you
I'll be there for you. This is not a drive
C♯m B A E
b - y - y - y - y. Just a shy guy look-ing for a two - ply
B G♯7/B♯ A
Hef - ty bag to hold my - y - y - y - y - y - y love. When you move me,
E B C♯m B
ev - 'ry-thing is groov - y. They don't like it, sue me. Mmm, the way you do me.

A
E
F♯m
To Coda
Oh, I swear to you I'll be there for you. This is not a drive
1
G♯
4fr
C♯m
4fr
2
G♯
4fr
by - y - y - y - y.
by - y - y - y - y.
G♯m7
4fr
C♯m
4fr
F♯m
Please be - lieve that when I leave
B
B/A
G♯
4fr
F♯m
there's noth - ing up my sleeve but love for you,

B7
B6/9
B5
and a lit - tle time to get my head to - geth - er, too.
C♯m
4fr
A
On the oth - er side of a street I knew stood a girl that looked like you.
E
B
D.S. al Coda
I guess that's dé - jà vu, but I thought, "This can't be true." 'Cause,
CODA
G♯
4fr
Asus2
by - y - y - y - y.

DROPS OF JUPITER
(Tell Me)

Words and Music by PAT MONAHAN,
JAMES STAFFORD, ROBERT HOTCHKISS,
CHARLES COLIN and SCOTT UNDERWOOD

F
hey,
hey hey,
C
she acts like sum - mer and walks like rain, re - minds
she checks out Mo - zart while she does Tae - Bo, re - minds
G
me that there's a time to change, hey
me that there's room to grow, hey
F
hey.
hey.
Since
Now that

C
G
the re - turn from her stay on the moon, she lis - tens like spring and she talks
she's back in the at - mos - phere I'm a - fraid that she might think
F
like June. Hey, hey, hey,
of me as plain old Jane, told a sto - ry 'bout a man who was
G
hey. (1., D.S.) But tell me, did you
too a - fraid to fly so he nev - er did land. (2.) But tell me, did the
G/A
D
C/E
sail a - cross the sun? Did you make it to the Milk - y Way
wind sweep you off your feet? Did you fi - n'lly get the chance to dance

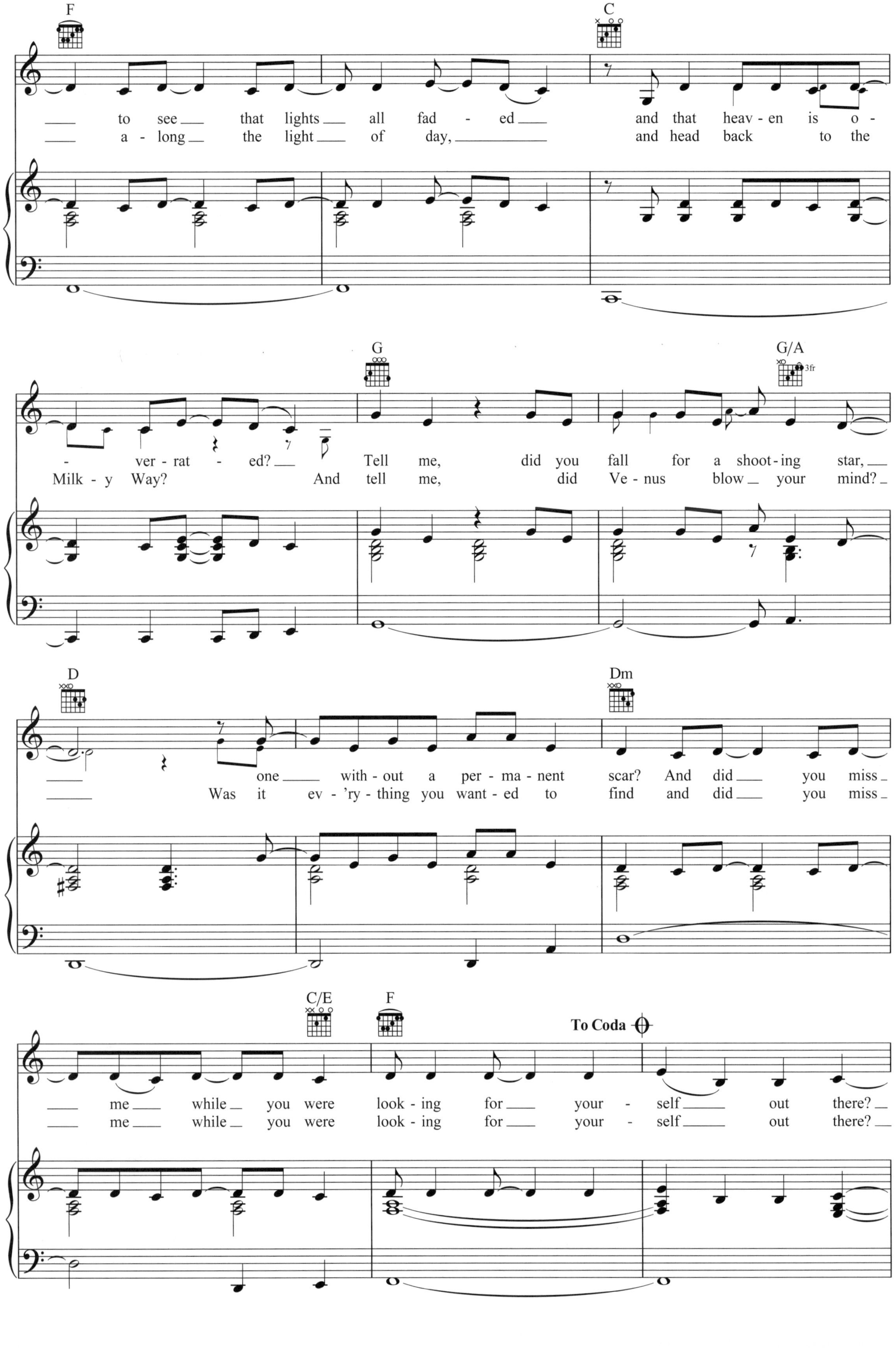
F
C
to see that lights all fad - ed and that heav - en is o -
a - long the light of day, and head back to the
G
G/A
3fr
- ver - rat - ed? Tell me, did you fall for a shoot - ing star,
Milk - y Way? And tell me, did Ve - nus blow your mind?
D
Dm
one with - out a per - ma - nent scar? And did you miss
Was it ev - 'ry - thing you want - ed to find and did you miss
C/E
F
To Coda
me while you were look - ing for your - self out there?
me while you were look - ing for your - self out there?

1
C
G7(no3rd)/D
3fr
G5
3fr
Fsus2
Now that _
2
C
G5
3fr
Fsus2

C
Can you i - mag - ine no love, pride, deep - fried chick - en, your
G
Fsus2
best friend al - ways stick - ing up for you,
F7sus2
Gsus
3fr
e - ven when I know you're wrong? Can you i - mag - ine no
C
G5
3fr
first dance, freeze - dried ro - mance, five - hour phone

B♭
C/B♭
con - ver - sa - tion, the best soy lat - te that you ev - er had ___ and
F
G
me? But tell me, did the
G/A
3fr
D
C/E
wind sweep you off your feet? ___ Did you fin - 'lly get the chance to dance ___
F
C
___ a - long ___ the light of day _______ and head back toward the

D.S. al Coda
CODA
N.C.
C
Milk - y Way? And self? Na na na
G
na na na na na na na na na na
F
na na na na. And did you fi - n'lly get the chance to dance a - long the light
C
of day? Na na na na na na

G
F
na na na na na na na na na na.
And did you fall from a
shoot - ing star, fall from a shoot - ing star?
C
G
Na na na na na na na na na
Bb
C/Bb
Bb
F
na na na.
And are you lone - ly look - ing for your - self out there?
rall.

50 WAYS TO SAY GOODBYE

Words and Music by PAT MONAHAN,
ESPEN LIND and AMUND BJØRKLUND

* *Recorded a half step lower.*

C
Am7
B7sus
2fr
I'll take the high road like I should.
Some - day I'll find a love like yours.
B7
Em
Am7
You said it's meant to be,
She'll think I'm Su - per - man,
D
G
C
that it's not you, it's me. You're leav - in' now
not su - per min - i - van. How could you leave
Am7
B7sus
2fr
B7
for my own good. That's
on Yom Kip - pur? That's

N.C.
C5
3fr
cool, but if my friends ask where you are, I'm gon-na say: She went down in an air-plane,
cool, but if my friends ask where you are, I'm gon-na say: She was caught in a mud-slide,
G5
D5
5fr
E5
fried get-tin' sun-tanned, fell in a ce-ment mix-er full of quick-sand.
eat-en by a li-on, got run o-ver by a crap-py pur-ple Sci-on.
F♯5
Help me, help me, I'm no good at good-byes.
Help me, help me, I'm no good at good-byes.
B
She met a shark un-der wa-ter, fell and no one caught her.
She dried up in the des-ert, drowned in a hot tub,

D5 E5 D5 C5
5fr 5fr 3fr
I re-turned ev-'ry-thing I ev-er bought her.
danced to death at an east-side night-club.
Help me, help me, I'm
G5 B5
3fr
all out of lies and ways to say you died.
1
Em Am7 D
G C Am7

B7sus
2fr
B7
2
Em
Am7
D
G
C
Am7
Bm
C
D5
5fr
I wan-na live a thou - sand lives with you. I wan-

C5
D5
3fr
5fr
- na be the one you're dy - in' to love,
C5
but you don't want to. That's
B5
N.C.
B5
cool, but if my friends ask where you are, I'm gon - na say... That's
cool, but if my friends ask where you are, I'm gon - na say: She went

C5
G5
3fr
down in an air - plane, fried get - tin' sun - tanned,
caught in a mud - slide, eat - en by a li - on,
D5
E5
D5
C5
5fr
fell in a ce - ment mix - er full of quick - sand. Help me, help me, I'm
got run o - ver by a crap - py pur - ple Sci - on. Help me, help me, I'm
G5
F#5
B
no good at good - byes. She met a
no good at good - byes. She dried
shark un - der wa - ter, fell and no one caught her.
up in the des - ert, drowned in a hot tub,

D5 E5 D5 C5
I re-turned ev-'ry-thing I ev-er bought her. Help me, help me, I'm
danced to death at an east-side night-club. Help me, help me, I'm
G5 1 B5
all out of lies. She was
all out of lies
2 B5 C5 G5 D5
and ways to say you died.
C5 G5 D5

GET TO ME

Words and Music by PAT MONAHAN,
SCOTT UNDERWOOD, JAMES STAFFORD,
CHARLES COLIN and ROBERT HOTCHKISS

to me.
Par - a - sail or first class mail,
get in the back of a Night - in - gale. Just get to me. I don't care, just get
to me.
D7sus
Pro Keds, mo - peds, take a lim - ou - sine in - stead.
Csus2
3fr
They ain't cheap but they're eas - y to find.
D7sus
Get on the high - way, point your - self my way.

Csus2
3fr
B♭sus2
Take a roll-er-coast-er that comes in side-ways. Just get to me, yeah.
C(add9)
Go on, hitch a ride on the back of a but-
D7sus
B♭(add9)
6fr
ter-fly. There's no bet-ter way to fly to get to me.
F6/9
C(add9)
I look a-round, what I got, and with-out you

Am7
B♭(add9)
6fr
it ain't a lot. But I got ev - 'ry - thing with you, ev -
To Coda
D7sus
'ry - thing.
C5
3fr
D7sus
C5
3fr
D7sus
3
Well, may - be you could pol - li - nate o - ver the Gold - en Gate. Take a

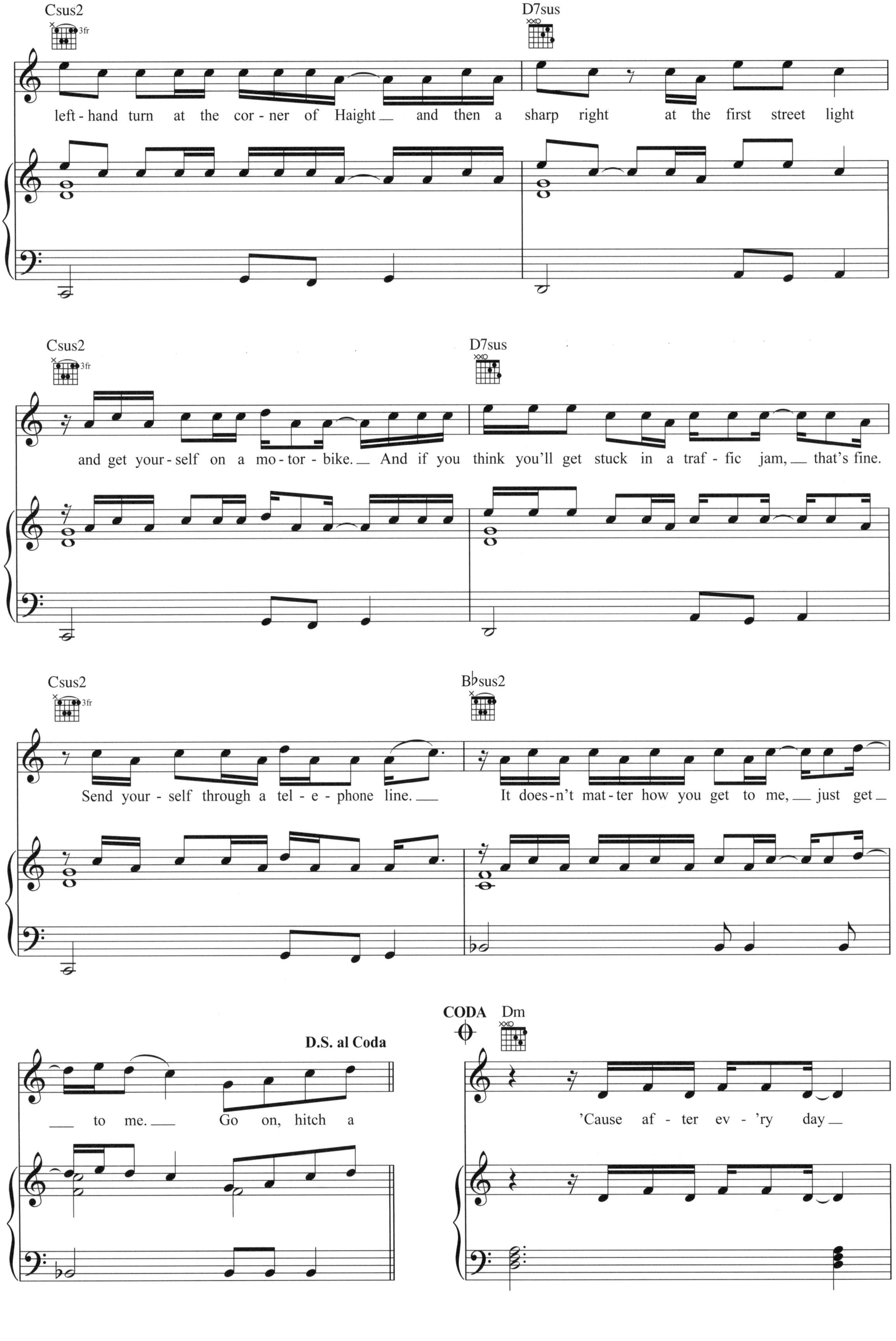
Csus2
3fr
D7sus
left - hand turn at the cor - ner of Haight and then a sharp right at the first street light
Csus2
3fr
D7sus
and get your - self on a mo - tor - bike. And if you think you'll get stuck in a traf - fic jam, that's fine.
Csus2
3fr
B♭sus2
Send your - self through a tel - e - phone line. It does - n't mat - ter how you get to me, just get
D.S. al Coda
to me. Go on, hitch a
CODA
Dm
'Cause af - ter ev - 'ry day

F/C
the wind blows the night - time my way.
B♭6
And I i - mag - ine that you are
Gm
a - bove me like a star.
F
And you keep on glow - ing,
F/A
and you keep on show - ing me the way.
Gm
And I i - mag - ine that you are
B♭sus2
a - bove me like a star,
Dm
shine,

Am7
B♭
shine,
shine.
Gm
C(add9)
Go on, hitch a ride on the back of a but-
D7sus
B♭sus2
ter - fly. There's no bet - ter way to fly to get to me.
F6/9
C(add9)
I look a - round, what I got, and with - out you

Am7
B♭6/9
it ain't a lot. But I got ev - 'ry - thing with you, ev -
1
2
- 'ry - thing. Go on, hitch a - 'ry - thing.
C(add9)
D7sus
And I got ev - 'ry - thing with you, ev -
B♭(add9)
6fr
F6/9
- 'ry - thing.

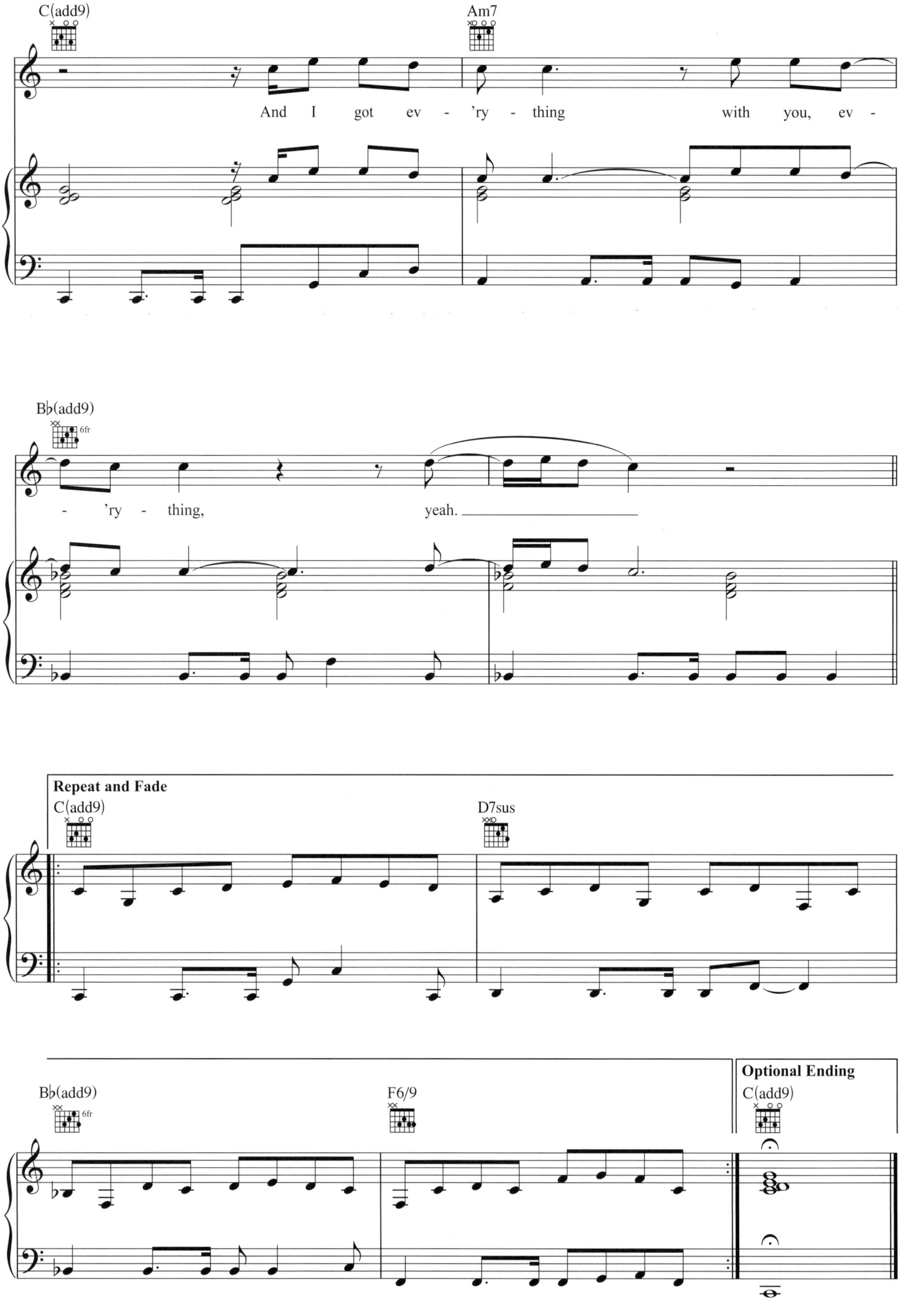
C(add9)
Am7
And I got ev - 'ry - thing with you, ev -
B♭(add9)
6fr
- 'ry - thing, yeah.
Repeat and Fade
C(add9)
D7sus
B♭(add9)
6fr
F6/9
Optional Ending
C(add9)

IF IT'S LOVE

Words and Music by PAT MONAHAN
and GREGG WATTENBERG

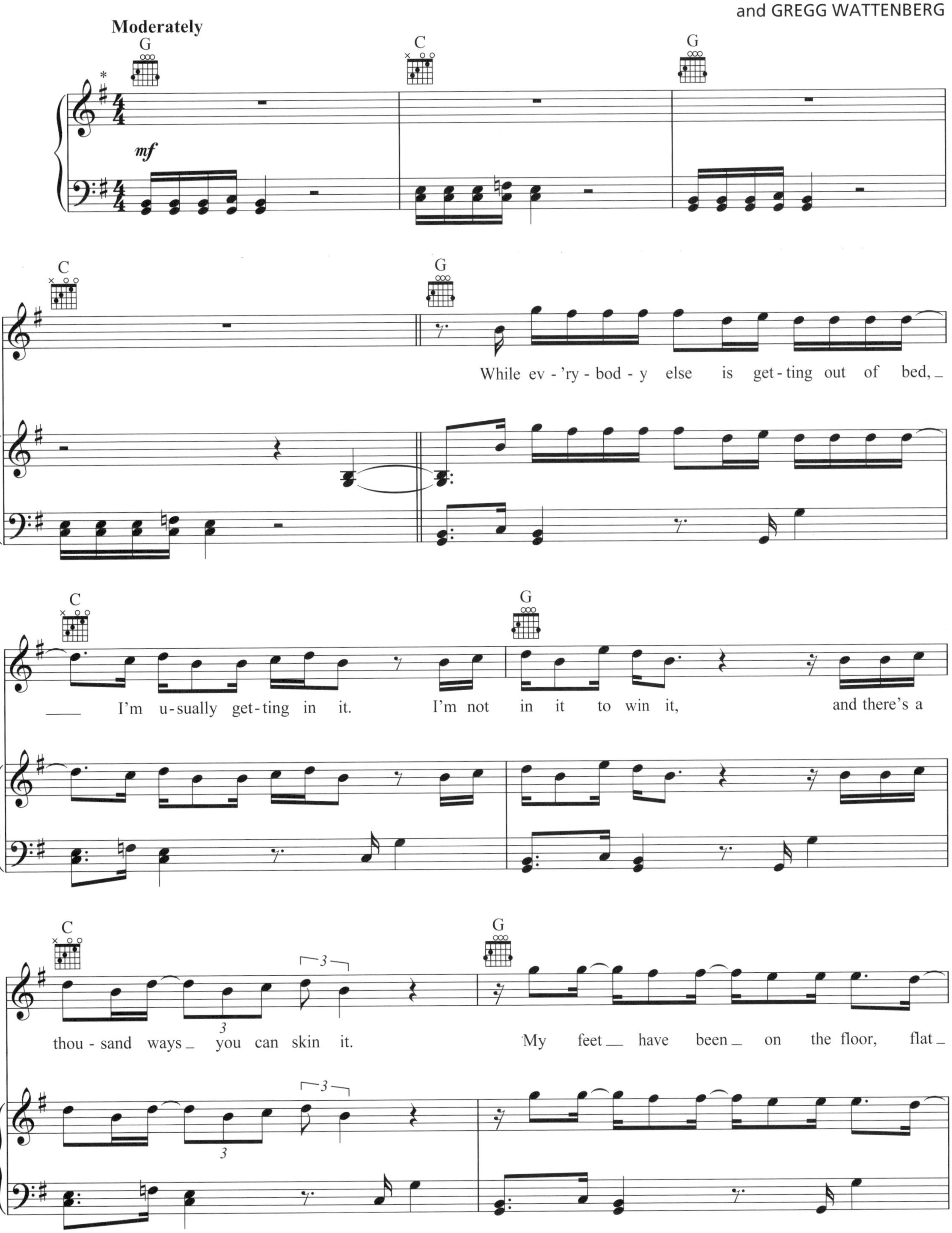

* *Recorded a half step lower.*

C
G
like an "I - dol" sing - er. Re-mem-ber Wing-er? I di-gress. I con -
C
G
fess, you are the best thing in my life. But I'm a - fraid when I hear sto -
C
Dsus
G
- ries 'bout hus-band and wife; there's no hap - py end - ings, no Hen - ry Lee. But you
D(add4)
G5
are the great-est thing a - bout me. If it's love

D(add4)/F♯
Em7
and we de - cide that it's for - ev - er, no one else
Csus2
Dsus
G5
D(add4)/F♯
could do it bet - ter. If it's love and we're two
Em7
Csus2
Dsus
birds of a feath - er, then the rest is just when - ev - er. And
G5
D(add4)/F♯
if I'm ad - dict - ed to lov - ing you and you're ad - dict - ed to my love, too,
3fr

Em7
Csus2
Dsus
we can be them two birds of a feath - er that flock to - geth - er.
G
Am7(add4)
G/B
C
Love, love; got to have some-thing to keep us to -
To Coda
G
Am7(add4)
G/B
C
geth - er. Love, love; that's e - nough for me.
G
C
Took a loan on a house I own; can't be a queen bee with - out a bee throne.

G
C
I wan-na buy you ev - 'ry - thing ex - cept co - logne, 'cause it's poi - son.
G
C
We can trav - el to Spain, where the rain falls main - ly on the plain. Sounds in - sane, 'cause it
G
C
is. We can laugh, we can sing, have ten kids and give 'em ev - 'ry - thing. Hold our
G
C
Dsus
cell phones up in the air and just be glad that we made it here a - live on a

G
G/F♯
D(add4)
D.S. al Coda
spin-ning ball in the mid-dle of space. I love you from your toes to your face.
3
3
CODA
G/B
C
Am7(add4)
You can move in; I won't ask where you've
that's e-nough for me.
Csus2
G5
been, 'cause ev - 'ry - bod - y has a past.
D(add4)/F♯
Am7(add4)
Csus2
When we're old - er, we'll do it all o - ver a - gain.

G
C
When ev-'ry-bod-y else is get-ting out of bed,
I'm u-sually get-ting in it. I'm not
G
C
D(add4)
3fr
G
in it to win it; I'm in it for you.
If it's love
D(add4)/F♯
Em7
and we're two birds of a feath - er, then the rest
Csus2
3fr
D5
5fr
G5
3fr
D(add4)/F♯
is just when-ev - er...

Em7
Csus2
Dsus
then the rest is just when-ev - er.
G5
D(add4)/F♯
If it's love and we de - cide
Em7
Csus2
Dsus
that it's for-ev - er, no one else could do it bet - ter. And
G5
D(add4)/F♯
if I'm ad-dict-ed to lov-ing you and you're ad-dict-ed to my love, too,

Em7
Csus2
Dsus
3fr
we can be them two birds of a feath - er that flock to-geth - er.
G
Am7(add4)
G/B
C
Love, love; got to have some-thing to keep us to -
geth - er. Love, love; got to have some-thing to keep us to -
G
Am7(add4)
G/B
C
G
geth - er. Love, love; that's e-nough for me.

HEY, SOUL SISTER

Words and Music by PAT MONAHAN,
ESPEN LIND and AMUND BJØRKLAND

B/D♯
C♯m
A
B
let you blow my mind. Your
E
B
sweet moon - beam, the smell of you in ev - 'ry
C♯m
A
sin - gle dream I dream, I knew when we col - lid -
E
B
- ed you're the one I have de - cid - ed who's one of my kind.

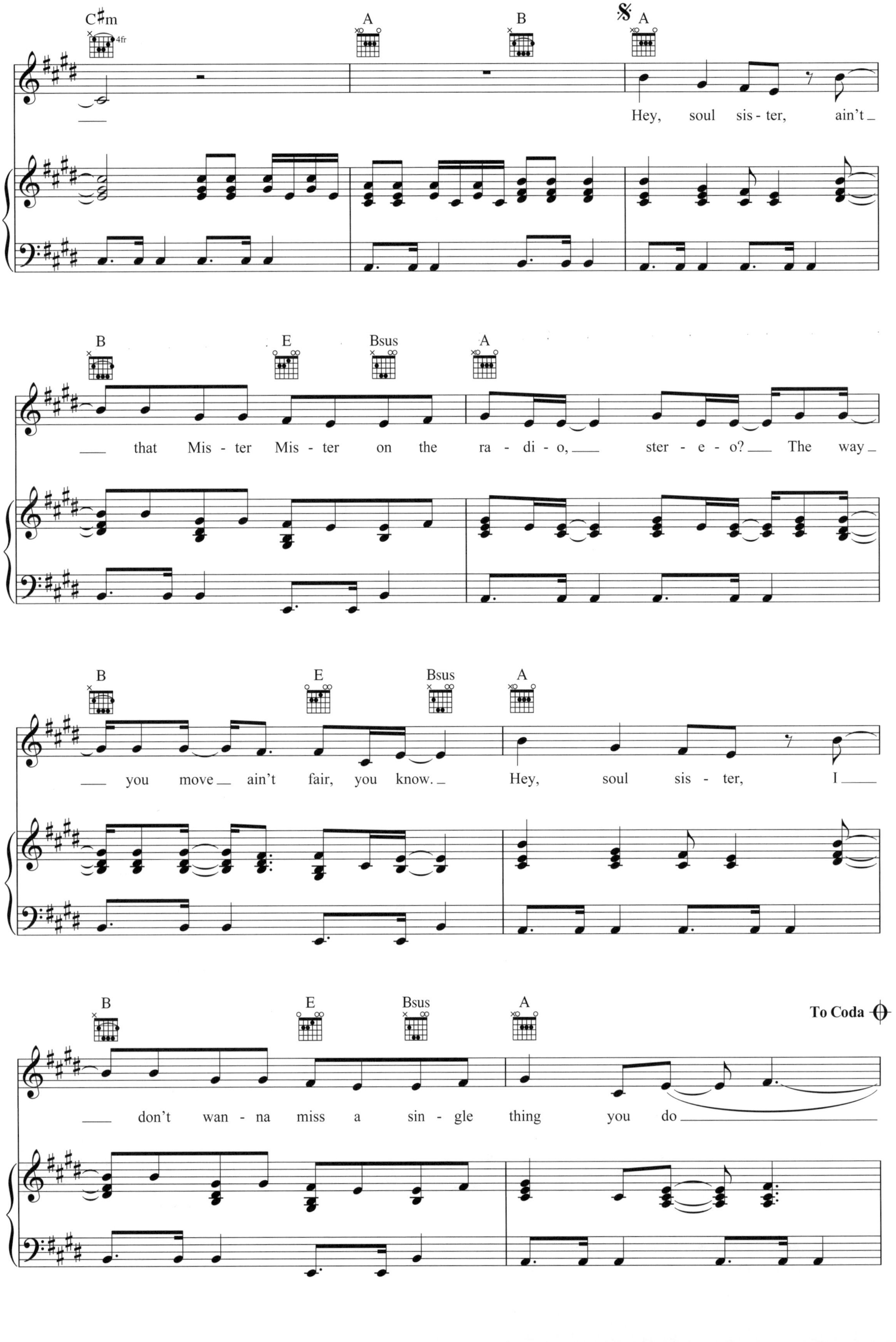
C♯m
A
B
A
Hey, soul sis - ter, ain't
B
E
Bsus
A
that Mis - ter Mis - ter on the ra - di - o, ster - e - o? The way
B
E
Bsus
A
you move ain't fair, you know. Hey, soul sis - ter, I
B
E
Bsus
A
To Coda
don't wan - na miss a sin - gle thing you do

B
E
B
to - night.
Hey,
hey,
C♯m
A
hey!
E
B
Just in time,
I'm so glad you have a
C♯m
A
one - track mind like me.
You gave my life di - rec -

E
B
- tion, a game - show love con - nec - tion we can't de -
C♯m
A
B
E
4fr
ny. I, I, I, I'm so ob - sessed.
B
C♯m
4fr
My heart is bound to beat right out my un - trimmed chest.
A
E
I be - lieve in you. Like a vir - gin, you're Ma - don -

B
C♯m
A
B
D.S. al Coda
- na, and I'm al - ways gon-na wan - na blow_ your mind._
CODA
B
E
_ to - night._ The way you can cut a rug,_
B
C♯m
watch-ing you's_ the on - ly drug_ I need._ Some gang-sta, I'm_ so thug,_ you're the
A/C♯
E/B
on - ly one_ I'm dream - ing of._ You see,_ I can be my - self_ now fi - nal - ly._

B
C♯m
C♯m/B
In fact, there's noth-in' I can't be. I want the world to see you'll
A
Bsus
A
B
E
Bsus
be with me. Hey, soul sis-ter, ain't that Mis-ter Mis-ter on the
A
B
E
Bsus
ra-di-o, ster-e-o? The way you move ain't fair, you know.
A
B
E
Bsus
A
Hey, soul sis-ter, I don't wan-na miss a sin-gle thing you do to-night.

B
Esus2
Bsus
A
Hey, soul sis - ter, I
B
E
Bsus
A
B
don't wan - na miss a sin - gle thing you do to - night.
E
B
C♯m
4fr
Hey, hey, hey,
1
2
A
B7sus
2fr
E5
to - night.
to - night.

MARRY ME

Words and Music by DAVID KATZ,
PAT MONAHAN and SAM HOLLANDER

Am7
Gsus
3fr
Fsus2
feel like I've had long e - nough with you.
feel like I am close e - nough to you.
C
For - get the world now,
You wear white, and
Gsus/B
G/B
Am7
we won't let them see.
But there's
I'll wear out the words "I love you"
Gsus
3fr
Fsus2
one thing left to do:
and "you're beau - ti - ful."

C/E
Fsus2
Now that the weight has lift - ed,
Now that the wait is o - ver
C/E
love has sure - ly
and love has fi - n'lly
Fsus2
shift - ed my way,
showed her my way,
C
mar - ry me,
Gsus/B
G/B

Am7
Gsus
3fr
Fsus2
to - day ___ and ev - 'ry ___ day. ___
C
Mar - ry
Gsus/B
G/B
Am7
me. If I ev - er get ___ the nerve _
Gsus
3fr
Fsus2
___ to say ___ "hel - lo" ___ in this ___ ca -

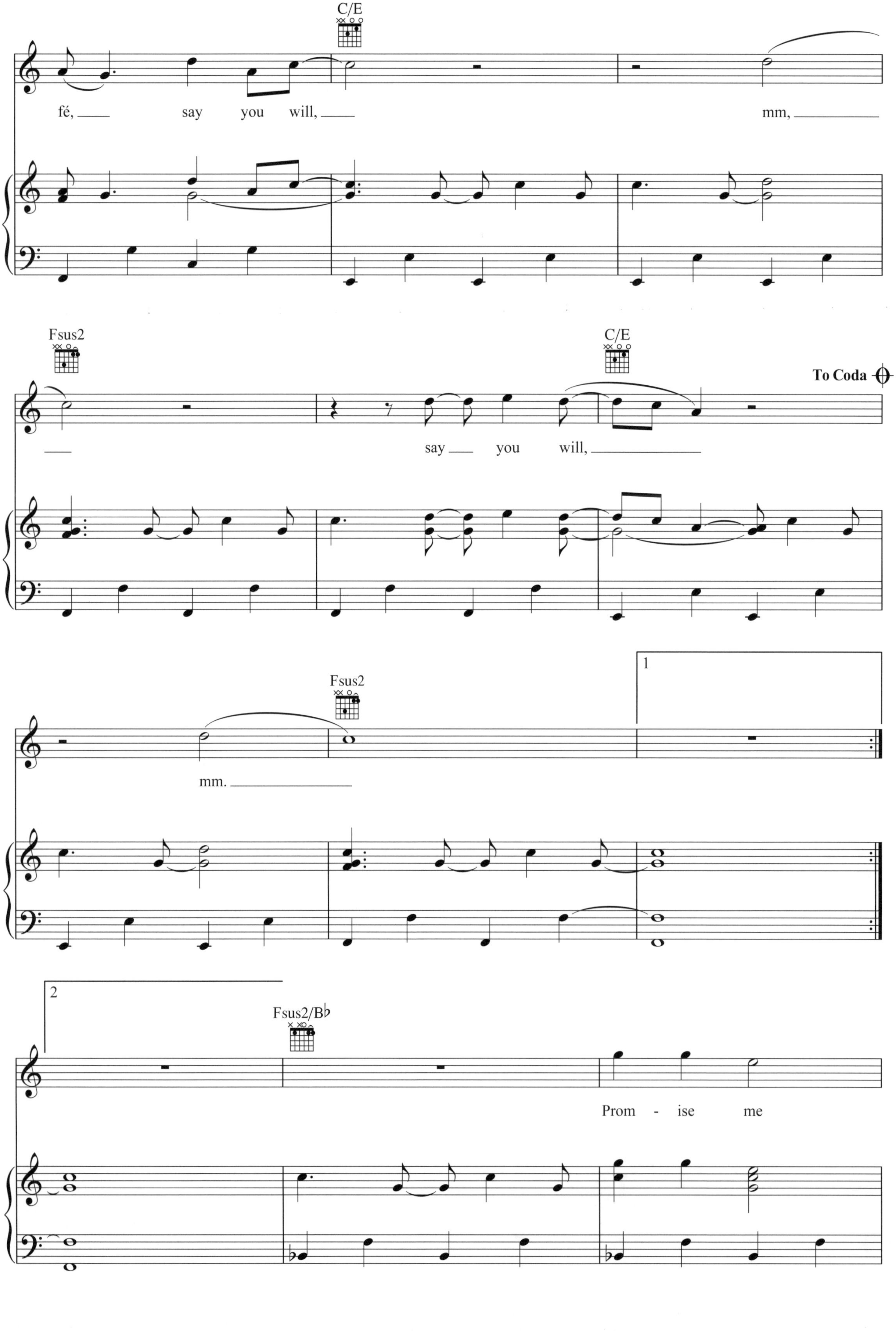
C/E
fé, say you will, mm,
Fsus2
C/E
To Coda
say you will,
Fsus2
mm.
1
2
Fsus2/B♭
Prom - ise me

Fsus2/A
C
you'll al - ways be
Gsus/B
G/B
hap - py by my side.
Fsus2/B♭
Fsus2/A
I prom - ise to sing
C
to you
when all the mu - sic

Gsus/B
G/B
Fsus2/B♭
dies.
Fsus2/A
D.S. al Coda
And
CODA
Fsus2
mm,
mar - ry
C/E
Fsus2
me,
mm.

MEET VIRGINIA

Words and Music by PAT MONAHAN,
JAMES STAFFORD, ROBERT HOTCHKISS,
CHARLES COLIN and SCOTT UNDERWOOD

A5 Dsus G5 C5
5fr 3fr 3fr
A5 Dsus/F♯ G5 C5 C/D
She nev - er com - pro - mis - es,
Well, here she is a - gain on the
A5 Dsus G5 C5 C/B
loves ba - bies and sur - pris - es, wears high heels when she ex - er - cis - es.
phone. Just like me, hates to be a - lone. We just like to sit home
A5 N.C. G5 C5
Ain't that beau - ti - ful? Meet Vir - gin - ia.
and rip on the pres - i - dent. Meet Vir - gin - ia.

A5
5fr
Dsus/F♯
Em
Well, she wants
Well, she wants
C
D(add4)
3fr
Em
to be the queen and she thinks
to live her life and she thinks
C
Em/B
Em
a - bout her scene,
a - bout her life,
pulls her hair
C
D(add4)
3fr
Em
To Coda
back as she screams,
"I don't real -

C
Dsus(add2)
G5
C
C/D
ly wan - na be the queen."
Her dad - dy wres - tles al - li - ga - tors.
A5
D5
C5
G5
Ma - ma works on car - bu - re - tors.
Broth - er is a fine
C5
C/B
A5
D5
C5
D.S. al Coda
med - i - a - tor for the pres - i - dent.
CODA
Csus2
D(add4)
Em
"I don't real - ly wan - na live this life."

Cmaj7
Em
No, no.
(Vocal 1st time only)
1 Cmaj7
2 Cmaj7
D(add4)
No, no.
No, no.
G5
C5
A5
N.C.
N.C.
G5
N.C.
A5
A5/G
D5
G
C5
C/B
A5
She on - ly drinks cof - fee at mid - night when the
You see, her con - fi - dence is trag - ic, but her

D5 C5 G5 C5 C/B
mo - ment is not right and the tim - ing is quite
in - tu - i - tion mag - ic and the shape of her bod -
A5 1 Dsus 2 Dsus/F♯ N.C.
un - u - su - al.
y un - u - su - al. Meet Vir - gin -
- ia. I can't wait to meet Vir - gin - ia, yeah, yeah,
Em C
hey, hey, hey. Well, she wants to be
Well, she wants to live

D(add4)
Em
C
Em/B
3fr
the queen and she thinks a - bout her scene.
her lives, and she thinks a - bout
Em/B
Em
C
D(add4)
her lives. Pulls her hair back as she screams,
Em
C
Dsus/B
Em
"I don't real - ly wan - na be the queen. I,
C
D(add4)
C
Dsus
I don't real - ly wan - na be the queen. I ly wan - na live a dream."
rit.

MERMAID

Words and Music by PAT MONAHAN,
ESPEN LIND, AMUND BJØRKLUND,
TOR HERMANSEN and MIKKEL ERIKSEN

B♭ Cm Gm
took a boat to an is - land so re - mote
A♭ B♭ Cm
on - ly John - ny Depp has ev - er been to it be - fore.
E♭/G A♭ B♭
I stayed there till the air was clear.
Cm Gm Fm
I was bored and out of tears, then I saw you washed

B♭
G7
up on the shore.
A♭
B♭
Cm
4fr
3fr
I of - fered you my coat; thank God its love
Sharks green with en - vy, they won - der what you see
Gm
A♭
B♭
3fr
4fr
can float. Cra - zy how that ship - wreck meant my
in me. Fun - ny, but some - times, can't help but
Cm
E♭/G
A♭
3fr
3fr
4fr
ship was com - ing in. We talked till the
won - der that as well. Now, life is a

B♭
Cm
Gm
sun went down; love on the Pu - get Sound.
hol - i - day, mak - ing up for the years I paid.
Fm
My treas - ure map was on your
The way to this heav - en - ly bay,
3
G7
Cm
skin.
it went through hell.
Beau - ty in the
A♭
E♭
B♭
Cm
wa - ter, an - gel on a beach. O - cean's
3fr
4fr

A♭
4fr
E♭
3fr
B♭
daugh - ter, I thought love was out of reach
Cm
3fr
A♭
4fr
E♭
3fr
till I got her. Had I
B♭
Fm
Fm(add4)
known it could come true, I would have wished in nine - ty - two
G7
To Coda
A♭
4fr
for a mer - maid just

B♭ Cm Gm A♭
like you, (Whoa.) just
1 B♭ Cm Gm
like you. (Whoa.)
2 B♭
like
Cm Gm B♭
you. (Whoa.) Res - cued you by the
Fm
ban - yan tree. All the girl - fish in the sea

A♭
4fr
could - n't hold a can - dle to you. They don't have a han - dle on you.
E♭
3fr
C♭
They don't have a scan - dal on you. I love Ec - co san - dals on you.
B♭
Fm
Sav - ing me was B - I - G. All the boy - fish
A♭
4fr
in the sea, they all wish that they could be me.

G7
A♭
Can't swim, so I
B♭
Cm
Gm
took a boat to an is - land so re - mote
A♭
B♭
Cm
on - ly John - ny Depp has ev - er been to it be - fore.
G7
D.S. al Coda
Oh!

CODA
A♭
4fr
mer - maid just
B♭
Cm
3fr
Gm
3fr
like you, (Whoa.)
A♭
4fr
B♭
Cm
3fr
just like you. (Whoa.)
1
Gm
3fr
2
Gm
3fr
A♭maj7

THIS AIN'T GOODBYE

Words and Music by PAT MONAHAN
and RYAN TEDDER

Moderately slow
F5 F5/G Dm7 B♭sus2 F5 F5/G
3fr
mf
With pedal
Dm7 Dm F5 F5/G
You and I were friends from out - er space,
We were stars up in the sun - lit sky
Dm7 B♭sus2 F5 F5/G
a - fraid to let go; the on - ly two who un - der - stood this place.
that no one else could see. Nei - ther of us thought to ev - er ask why
Dm7 B♭sus2 F5 F5/G
And as far as we know, we were way be - fore our time,
it was - n't meant to be. May - be we were way too high

* *Recorded a half step higher.*

Dm7
B♭sus2
F5
F5/G
3fr
as bold as we were blind.
Just an-oth-er per-fect mis-
to ev-er un-der-stand.
May-be we were vic-tims of
Dm7
B♭sus2
Gm
3fr
F
take, an-oth-er bridge to take
on the way to let-ting go.
all, all the fool-ish plans
we be-gan to di-vide.
C
F
Gm7(add4)
This ain't good-bye;
But this ain't good-bye;
this is just where love goes
Dm7
B♭(add2)
3fr
F
Gm7(add4)
when words aren't warm e-nough
to keep a-way the cold.

Dm7
C
F
Gm7(add4)
Oh, no, this ain't good - bye; it's not where our sto - ry ends.
Dm7
B♭(add2)
3fr
F
Gm7(add4)
To Coda
But I know you can't be mine, not the way you've al - ways been.
Dm7
C
Dm7
C
As long as we've got time,
1
B♭maj9
5fr
F5
F5/G
3fr
then this ain't good - bye.

Dm7
B♭sus2
F5
F5/G
Oh, no, this ain't good - bye.
Dm7
C7sus
2
B♭maj9
N.C.
this ain't good - bye.
F
Gm7(add4)
Dm7
Csus
3fr
Oh, no, this ain't good - bye. Oh, oh.
F
Gm7(add4)
Dm7
C
Oh, no, this ain't good-bye.

F
Gm7(add4)
Dm7
Csus
3fr
No no no, no no no. No no no no no no no.
F
Gm7(add4)
Dm7
C
No no no, this ain't good - bye.
B♭(add2)
3fr
B♭sus2
F5
F5/G
3fr
You and I were friends from out - er space,
Dm7
B♭sus2
F5
F5/G
3fr
a - fraid to let go; the on - ly two who un - der - stood this place.

Dm7
B♭sus2
And as far as we know, this ain't good - bye.
F
Gm7(add4)
Dm7
B♭(add2)
3fr
Oh no, this ain't good - bye. This ain't good - bye;
F
Gm7(add4)
Dm7
C
D.S. al Coda
oh no, this ain't good - bye. This ain't good - bye;
CODA
Dm7
C
F
Gm7(add4)
Oh no, I'm sing - ing: No no no, no no no.

Dm7
B♭(add2)
3fr
F
Gm7(add4)
No no no no no no no.
No no no, don't say good - bye.
Dm7
C
C(add4)
N.C.
B♭maj9
5fr
rit.

WHEN I LOOK TO THE SKY

Words and Music by PAT MONAHAN,
SCOTT UNDERWOOD, JAMES STAFFORD
and CHARLIE COLIN

F/C
C
F/C
C
ships we sink our lips in - to the ones we love that have to say good - bye.
G5
3fr
Fsus2
C/E
And as I float a - long this o -
And while I float up - on this o -
Dm9
3fr
Fsus2
C/E
- cean I can feel you like a no -
- cean I can feel you like a no -
E♭
3fr
G/D
C
- tion that won't seem to let me go.
- tion that I hope will nev - er leave.
'Cause when I look to the sky

G
Fmaj9
some - thing tells me you're here with me. And you make
Am
B♭sus2
C
G
ev - 'ry - thing al - right. But when I feel like I'm lost some - thing tells me you're here
Fmaj9
To Coda
Am
B♭sus2
with me. And I can al - ways find my way when you are here.
C
Cmaj7
F/C
C
F
C

G
C
Cmaj7
And ev - 'ry word _ I did - n't say _
F/C
C
F
C
_ caught _ up in _ some bus - y day. _ And ev - 'ry dance _ on the kitch - en floor _
G
C
Cmaj7
_ we did - n't have be - fore. And ev - 'ry sun - set that we'll
F/C
C
F
C
miss, I'll wrap them all _ up in a kiss _ and pick you up _ in all _ of this _

G
D.S. al Coda
CODA
Am
B♭sus2
when I sail a - way.
al - ways find my way.
F
G
Wheth - er I am up or down, or in, or out, or just plain o - ver - head
F/A
B♭sus2
in - stead, it feels like it's im - pos - si - ble to fly. But
F
G
with you I can spread my wings to see me o - ver ev - 'ry - thing that

Fmaj9
Am
B♭sus2
with me.
And you make ev - 'ry - thing al - right.
And I can al - ways find my way when you are here.
C
G
Dm9
3fr
When I feel like I'm lost some-thing tells me you're here with me.
And I can
Am
B♭sus2
C
al - ways find my way when you are here.

F/A
Bbsus2
life may send me when I'm hop - ing it won't pass me by.
D
A
And when I feel like there's no one that will ev - er know
Gmaj7
me, there you are to show me.
C
G
When I look to the sky some - thing tells me you're here